THE GOLDEN BUTTERFLY

An Interactive Angelic Experience

GINA CASEY

BALBOA.
PRESS

A DIVISION OF HAY HOUSE

Balboa Press books may be ordered through booksellers or by contacting:

Balboa Press
A Division of Hay House
1663 Liberty Drive
Bloomington, IN 47403
www.balboapress.com
1 (877) 407-4847

Because of the dynamic nature of the Internet, any web addresses or links contained in this book may have changed since publication and may no longer be valid. The views expressed in this work are solely those of the author and do not necessarily reflect the views of the publisher, and the publisher hereby disclaims any responsibility for them.

The author of this book does not dispense medical advice or prescribe the use of any technique as a form of treatment for physical, emotional, or medical problems without the advice of a physician, either directly or indirectly. The intent of the author is only to offer information of a general nature to help you in your quest for emotional and spiritual well-being. In the event you use any of the information in this book for yourself, which is your constitutional right, the author and the publisher assume no responsibility for your actions.

Any people depicted in stock imagery provided by Thinkstock are models, and such images are being used for illustrative purposes only. Certain stock imagery © Thinkstock.

Print information available on the last page.

ISBN: 978-1-5043-7914-4 (sc)
ISBN: 978-1-5043-7915-1 (e)

Library of Congress Control Number: 2017907599

Balboa Press rev. date: 06/12/2017

CONTENTS

I

INTRODUCTION

I created this book for you, yes you! I was once a lot like you, with so many questions, but not sure who to turn to for advice. It wasn't until many years later that I discovered how very loved and supported I am by the Archangels...and so are you! This magical realization opened up a whole new world of possibilities for me that I had never known before. I wish I had known, when I was your age, that I have an entire team of angels on my side, no matter what, How incredible is that!

My wish for you is that, by using this book for guidance whenever and wherever you'd like to, you get to know your personal team of angels even more closely.

The Archangels are gifts from God. They are His Heavenly messengers, who are with you always, no matter what your religious beliefs are. But here's the catch... Because God gave you free will, he respects your right to make your own choices. So when you need some extra support (and believe me, we ALL do sometimes), you just need to ask. Ask the Archangels, who are always ready, and more than willing to guide you in every single way.

I hope that by now, you are just as excited as I am to invite these beautiful, amazing angels into your life! So let's get started by taking three slow, deep breaths in, then out. Now focus on your topic. It could be something specific like school, a friend, a family member, a job, etc., or you might just be looking for some general guidance today; In this case, just think in your head, or say out loud "my message". Then think or say "Angels please come in and connect with me now."

The next step is choosing your images. There are sixteen in total. Fifteen of them represent Archangels. One image represents your Guardian Angel (who has been with you since the day you were born). While looking at the Table of Symbols, simply choose your first image from the vertical line of the table. Next, pick out your second image from the horizontal line. No need to overthink your selections, just go with your gut! Locate the point where your two images meet. This number will lead you to your message. Find this number in your book to receive your angelic guidance.

Always remember to thank your angels! An attitude of gratitude will surely strengthen your connection with the angelic realm.

You may now wish to write about your experience in the journal located at the back of your book. Don't forget to include the date, your topic, and the angels' messages. Journaling will help you to remember your angel messages, and see how your answers to the same topic may change day by day, week by week, etc.

You are loved.
You are blessed.
Happy Angel Journeys!

The images are as follows:

1. *dandelion*
2. *father hugging children*
3. *colors of the rainbow*
4. *moon landscape*
5. *boy with skinned knee*
6. *sky*
7. *candles*
8. *flower*
9. *owl*
10. *father & daughter holding hands*
11. *cosmos*
12. *heart*
13. *dove*
14. *waterfall*
15. *thumbs up*
16. *golden butterfly*

II

HOW TO GET YOUR MESSAGES

1. Take 3 slow deep breaths in, then out.
2. Focus on a topic that you would like guidance with.
3. Pick your first image from the vertical line of the Table of Images.
4. Pick your second symbol from the horizontal line of the Table of Images.
5. Find the number where the two images meet.
6. Turn to this numbered message in your book.
7. Read your message.
8. Thank your angels!
9. Record your message.

III

TABLE OF IMAGES

While focusing on your topic, first pick an image from the vertical (top to bottom) line. Then pick an image from the horizontal (across) line. Next, find the number where the two images meet. Find that numbered message in your book to receive your angels' guidance.

	1	2	3	4	5	6	7	8
	9	10	11	12	13	14	15	16
	1	2	3	4	5	6	7	8
	9	10	11	12	13	14	15	16
	1	2	3	4	5	6	7	8
	9	10	11	12	13	14	15	16
	1	2	3	4	5	6	7	8
	9	10	11	12	13	14	15	16

IV

MESSAGES

1

KEEP THE PEACE

Let there be peace on Earth, and let it begin with you.
Love,
Archangel Gabriel

2

YOU ARE SAFE

Protection and love I send from above. Receive
them now on the wings of a dove.
Love,
Archangel Michael

3

LET GO OF WORRY

Know that you belong. Know that you are strong.
Ask me for signs and I'll send before long.
Love,
Archangel Raziel

4

REMEMBER TO PRAY

Look up at the moon and say a prayer. I
will be waiting for you up there.
Love,
Archangel Haniel

5

YOU ARE HEALTHY

Your wounds I heal. No longer will you feel. I
am the doctor with Heaven's blessed seal.
Love,
Archangel Raphael

6

YOU ARE PROTECTED

I watch over you from the skies above and
send you all of Heaven's pure love.
Love,
Archangel Azrael

7

YOU ARE POWERFUL

Shine your light for all to see. It
reaches throughout eternity.
Love,
Archangel Uriel

8

YOU ARE BEAUTIFUL

In your heart lies beauty and joy. Share these
great gifts with each girl and boy.
Love,
Archangel Jophiel

9

YOU ARE WISE

You are wise beyond your years. Focus
on love. I will take your fears.
Love,
Archangel Metatron

10

ALL IS WELL

Take my hand and I will guide you.
All is well. I am beside you.
Love,
Archangel Jeremiel

11

YOU HAVE THE ANSWER

If you seek, you will find. Share what
you learn, and always be kind.
Love,
Archangel Zadkiel

12

SHARE YOUR LOVE

Feel all the love that you have in your heart. It will
always be there, and it's meant to be shared.
Love,
Archangel Chamuel

13

YOU CAN DO IT

Take my wings. I'll help you fly- to
Heaven above- just you and I.
Love,
Archangel Ariel

14

YOU ARE PEACEFUL

I'll help you live in harmony.If you're looking for peace, just call on me.
Love,
Archangel Raguel

15

YOU ARE BLESSED

I send you gifts from Heaven above.
The greatest one of all is love.
Love,
Archangel Sandalphon

16

YOU ARE MAGICAL

Magic, miracles and blessings surround
you wherever you go.
Love,
Your Guardian Angel

V

JOURNAL

DATE	TOPIC	MESSAGE

DATE	TOPIC	MESSAGE

DATE	TOPIC	MESSAGE

DATE	TOPIC	MESSAGE

DATE	TOPIC	MESSAGE

Printed in the United States
By Bookmasters